IF AT FIRST YOU DON'T SUCCEED, BUY THIS BOOK!

Catalyst Books
13 New Row
Covent Garden, London
WC2N 4LF
Tel: 0207 380 4646
info@catalystbooks.com

ISBN: 0-9629230-3-6

Copy editing by B2B Content Solutions, Incorporated
Cover design by Foster and Foster, Inc.

PRINTED BY THE BATH PRESS, BATH

IF AT FIRST YOU DON'T SUCCEED, BUY THIS BOOK!

Turbo Charge Your Life for

Greater Performance!

Power Principles for Achieving

Maximum Success

By:

David P. Schloss

Dedication

To my mom:

Thank you for all your love and guidance,

and for the constant encouragement

to always follow my dreams.

About the author...

Dave Schloss is an internationally acclaimed author whose motivational products inspire people to reach their personal best. He has made a career out of helping others achieve their goals; first, as a real estate instructor and trainer who helped many individuals launch successful real estate careers and later as a financial consultant and investment adviser showing many others the way to financial independence. He has also presented numerous motivational seminars and is a frequent guest on radio programs across the country, where he shares his winning ideas and inspires listeners to achieve more successful lives.

Dave is President of Motivation Plus, Inc., which is based in Pompano Beach, Florida and produces all of his motivational and investment products.

Also by David P. Schloss

- Don't Tie Yourself Up In "Nots"

- Don't Just Stand There..!

- Grow Your Own Money Tree!

Introduction

If at First You Don't Succeed, Buy This Book!
What kind of title is that for a book? I will admit, it's a
little different. But there is a method to my madness.

The cliché of course, is to "try, try again." Many
times, however, people *do* try again and again only to
get the same results. And if these results are not what
they want, it doesn't make a lot of sense to keep going
in the same direction. After all, doing the same things
over and over again while expecting different results is
one of the definitions of insanity.

What is very often needed for success to occur
is to apply different thought processes or strategies.
That's why some people succeed while others fail and
why some are prosperous while others are penniless.
The successful people have made the necessary
adjustments.

I wrote this book to re-establish many of the
seemingly forgotten "power principles" for success that
separate the winners from the non-winners in life. We
live in a fast-paced, high-tech world. Everything seems
more complicated today than ever before. But the basic

elements to winning and succeeding in life have not really changed.

Motivation is great and necessary, but it is not everything. You can have all the enthusiasm and motivation in the world but with the wrong strategies, goals and objectives, you will get no closer to what you want in life. You will simply be very motivated as you head in the wrong direction.

To really have long-term positive effects in your life, you must change the way you think. The goal of this book is to inspire the reader to view and react to situations in life differently. This new vantage point can help create long-lasting benefits and lifelong success.

We all need "focused motivation" to succeed. We need a plan and we need to implement it with all the energy we can muster. So, if at first you don't succeed, read on!

Tips on how to read this book

In today's fast-paced world, the need to disseminate information and determine what is important to us is critical. This book was written in an easy-to-read format to convey maximum benefit in the shortest amount of time while enabling the reader to apply its benefits immediately.

There are of course, different types of readers. There are the "nibblers" who like to read a little bit, come back later and read a little more. There are the moderate readers who take their time, as well as the voracious ones who will read the entire book in one sitting. You also have the "midnight snackers" who like to re-read little tidbits to get re-focused and re-energized. The Power Principles found throughout this book are perfect for everyone, especially the "midnight snackers."

There is no wrong way to read this book. I believe so strongly that these thoughts and ideas can help improve your life, the only way this book won't help you is if you don't open it!

TABLE OF CONTENTS

Chapter 1

ATTITUDE OF A CHAMPION

Maybe I should have titled the chapter, "FAILURE IS GOOD." Because the truth is, failing has a lot to do with winning. Of course, so does perseverance.

When many people hear the word "failure" they think it's the end, instead of what it really is, experience.

Power Principle
"You will never succeed if you are afraid to fail."
Put your trust in your beliefs, not your fears."

To be successful we have to look at failure and setbacks as just other ways to learn. No one gets through life without making mistakes and having setbacks. But it's critical to remember that these setbacks are there for us to learn from, not to focus on.

Power Principle
"If you aren't making mistakes,
you aren't making progress!"

I've always felt giving up was not an option because I didn't like the answer I received when I asked myself, "What will I have if I quit?"

Or for you analytical types, run a cost/results analysis. Ask yourself, "What will it cost me to try?" and "What are the potential results if I do?" More times than not, you will find that you have nothing to lose and everything to gain.

If you see failure as a door that has been closed, find a new one to open. If you see failure as a road that is closed, find a detour! But whatever you do, find a way.

I know of almost no one who ever succeeded in a big way on the first try. In 1962 a major record company told *The Beatles* they didn't like their sound and that groups with guitars were on the way out. As a sophomore in high school, Michael Jordan was cut from his high school basketball team. And how about Fred Smith? As a college junior he wrote a paper outlining the need for a nationwide delivery company specializing in time-sensitive goods. The paper got a C. Today his company is called Federal Express.

The point I'm making is, when someone tells us we can't do something, instead of looking at it as a failure, at least leave room in your mind that he or she could be wrong! There is great pleasure in doing what others say can't be done.

When I wrote my first book, *Don't Tie Yourself Up In "Nots"* I was told by everyone I contacted in the publishing industry that it would not sell. I received enough rejection letters to wallpaper the entire inside of my home. Almost all of them were form letters. Several publishers, however, actually took the time to write personal letters describing the degree to which they disliked my book. It was clear that no one wanted to publish it.

I could have given up there, but I knew the book was good. So instead of going the usual route of trying to get a publisher, I changed my approach and started marketing it myself directly to companies and organizations. As of the date of this writing, it has sold well over 120,000 copies in numerous countries and several languages. I've also received wonderful endorsements from many top motivational speakers. Persistence pays off. So does the ability to change your approach.

When a door closes in front of you, it could be because your approach is wrong and needs to be fine-tuned. It could also be because the person closing the door is completely wrong! In the first example, a new approach is what is called for, not quitting. In the second example, breaking down the door might be appropriate. Do whatever it takes.

I am speaking of course, in the figurative sense. I don't want to hear that readers of this book are out breaking down doors. But you must believe with everything in your heart that you are right and will succeed. You must also believe that you are on the right track and will win as long as you stay persistent and don't quit. Never let your thoughts or the thoughts of others stop you from becoming what you want to be in life.

Power Principle
"What it takes to discourage you, is in direct correlation to the amount of belief you have in yourself."

Almost anyone can stay motivated for a month or two. Some can stay motivated for a year or two. But what separates the winners in life from all the others is that winners stay motivated for whatever time it takes to succeed. They refuse to quit.

Remember, the road to success is paved with the bricks of individual accomplishments created by setting goals, and improving one's self through reading books, as well as going to classes and seminars. Because before we can be successful, personal growth must happen. In other words, for our lives to improve, we must improve.

If we stop learning, we stop growing. To truly grow as an individual, you must constantly stretch beyond your comfort zone. Basically, you must do what successful people do. Learn to do the things that others won't, and you will eventually be able to do what others can't.

Power Principle

"Repetition is one of the keys to success. To accomplish what you want in life, make it a way of life."

Rules for success should not only be committed to memory, but also committed to life!

Your success or failure is not determined by what happens to you, but by how you react to what happens to you. Getting knocked down doesn't create a setback. The setback comes from not getting back up. For those who need an analogy, you don't drown by being submersed in water, you drown by staying there.

I believe most people do almost enough to win. I also believe that "should" is the enemy of "must." As long as we think, "I should do this" or "I should do that" we feel like we are at least doing something. The truth is, if we want to be successful, we need to talk and think in terms of what we "must" do.

Staying on course and persevering is not easy or everyone would be doing it. Imagine what the world would be like if everyone quit when things got tough. Half-finished buildings, partially built automobiles, and unfinished books are only some of the results we would have! (I was thinking about adding some blank pages here for effect, but you get my point.) Persistence is the great equalizer. People with more perseverance than talent often accomplish more than those with more talent than perseverance. Don't get me wrong, if you want to succeed, having talent is good. But having perseverance is better. In other words, it doesn't matter how *good* you are, just how *bad* you want it! There is nothing more common than unsuccessful people with talent. But don't you also know people who lack great talent in a particular area, but are successful because of pure determination?

When you have determination and passion in your life nothing can stop you. Success is just having your efforts outnumber your setbacks by one.

Power Principle
"Any improvement in our lives is meaningful, regardless of size. Great mountains are scaled by many small steps!"

Wanting to succeed and having the determination to succeed are two entirely different concepts. Allow me to share an example with you.

Suppose you are swimming underwater and get yourself caught on something. You *want* to free yourself. But as you run short of air, you begin to experience determination! Every time you head in a particular direction in life ask yourself, "Is this something I merely want, or am I determined and passionate about what I am doing?"

I don't believe that most people today are living their dreams. As I speak with people, it seems to me that most are just getting by. They're working, paying bills, wanting more, but are afraid to try something new. They don't realize that it is this attitude that is holding them back from something greater.

So they do the same things every day, getting deeper and deeper into ruts until they are so far down, they no longer see options, just barriers. The fear of change and trying something new creates the building blocks of these walls.

Fear is really an acronym for **F**alse **E**vidence **A**ppearing **R**eal. If you let fear stop you from becoming the person you really want to be, *you* are giving it power over your life!

Power Principle
"You control the life span of your fears.
Once you have disposed of them, your own greatness
is limited only by your imagination!"

Once your mind has been stretched by your imagination, it never goes back to its original dimension. Many people incorrectly believe it takes big changes *today* to make big changes in their *future*. As a result they never start because they believe the task is overwhelming. The truth is, it takes only small but consistent changes in your present direction to make large changes in your future destination.

Success means different things to different people. Those who appear to be behind in the race are many times running a different race entirely. That's why we need to remain unconcerned about what others think.

We have all seen people who have been "stopped cold" worrying about doing this or that because they are afraid someone won't like it. Well guess what? No matter what you do, someone is guaranteed not to like it. You can't please everyone, no matter what you do.

Even if you take a course to become the nicest person on the planet, there will always be someone who won't like you. If you become very rich and give all your money to charity, there will be someone who won't like it. So decide right now not to worry about what others think, just make sure you are pleased with you.

Dare to compete! Dare to succeed! Dare to dream! You stop being just one of the crowd the moment you dare to dream. "DARE" is an acronym too. It stands for **Do All Required to Excel.**

Simply put, compete, don't compare. Compete against yourself, don't compare your success with the success of others. Your own definition of success is what matters. I have always believed that success occurs when opportunity meets preparation. That's why the effort we put forth today is not wasted, even if it seems to yield no immediate results. That effort is part of the preparation stage that puts you at the door when opportunity knocks, or at least close enough to hear it!

Power Principle
**"Always be prepared for opportunity,
or it's opportunity lost!"**

It's winners who see opportunities when losers see only problems. It's winners who say, "I'll find a way," when losers say, "It can't be done." It's winners who expect success, when losers expect failure.

If you think you are beaten, you are. If you think you can't, you won't. But if you think you can, you will!

I believe we can beat most of the competition simply by showing up everyday and working hard. Remember, it doesn't matter where you begin, only where you finish.

Power Principle
**"Whatever your past has been,
you have a spotless future!"**

As long as you are still breathing, there is time for you to improve your attitude, and with it, the way you think about yourself and others.

Chapter 2

IT'S ALL IN HOW YOU LOOK AT IT

How you look at life will determine how successful you will become. It has been said that "attitude is everything" and I believe that our attitude is based solely on our viewpoints.

<u>Power Principle</u>
"Having real vision in life is "seeing"
things others don't, then accomplishing
what others can't or won't."

You have probably seen a professional tennis match on TV. What happens when one player aces the other? The player being aced moves to the other side of the court and awaits the next serve. Have you ever seen a player who was aced, stop the match and tell the umpire how unfair the game was because the other player had a better serve? Or that he or she is really having a bad day and they feel like the whole world is against them? Hardly!

Yet, when some people get aced in life, the first thing they do is complain about how unfair things are and then open their very own "excuse factories." What they should do is "step to the other side of the court," so to speak, and get ready to hit whatever life serves up next.

I don't know anyone who likes being aced, in tennis or life, but here's a news flash. It's over! Move on. You can't change it. Besides, it's not defeat, but rather your attitude toward defeat, that matters.

Defeat is never permanent unless *you* decide it is. If you get aced in tennis, do what the tennis pros do, step to the other side of the court. When you get aced in life, do what the pros in life do, get ready to deal with whatever is next.

All some people want to do, however, is make excuses. Unfortunately, if they make enough excuses, they run the risk of coming down with "excuse-itis." It's a type of reverse flu. It makes everyone else sick of the person who has it.

The problem with excuses is that they don't matter. Even though some are legitimate, most are not. Besides, your friends don't need to hear them and your adversaries don't believe them and/or don't care. Even after the excuse has been made, you are still left to deal with the exact same situation. Don't make excuses, don't complain, just continue to compete.

In life, you get to keep trying until *you* decide it's time to quit! All setbacks can be comebacks if looked at with the proper perspective.

Whether you are "frozen" by your complaints and excuses made when encountering the "aces" in your life, or whether you continue on, will depend entirely on your viewpoint.

Power Principle
"The only difference between stumbling blocks and stepping stones is the way you use them."

I was in a sushi restaurant a few weeks ago and I asked the chef, "How's it going today?" He replied rather negatively, "Oh, OK, I guess. Sometimes I get tired of doing the same thing everyday, making the same rolls and seeing these same walls." I suddenly wasn't very hungry.

More recently, I was back in the same restaurant

and there was a different chef on duty. I asked him the same question, "How's it going?" He looked at me and said, "Great, man! Why wouldn't it be? I get to work in the air conditioning, see all the beautiful women who come in, and at the same time I get to construct works of art!"

Which chef do you think will be the most successful? And I don't mean just as a chef, but throughout his entire life? Both these chefs are doing the same job in the same restaurant. One is unhappy while the other is having the time of his life.

Our viewpoint determines our degree of happiness. One reason many people today are unhappy or unfulfilled is because they spend a great deal of time searching for things they believe will bring them happiness. The problem is, "things" don't bring happiness. Happiness has to come from the inside, launched first by a positive viewpoint. Nothing can bring you happiness if you are not first happy with who you are. The list is long of people who seemingly "had it all" only to take their own lives.

Another reason people are unhappy is that they fail to get their priorities straight. Some people find their priorities don't change as they go through life, no matter how much their circumstances may change. Others see a slow change over a period of years, some change more quickly, while a few will see their priorities change almost immediately in response to what life throws at us. It all depends on... that's right... your viewpoint!

For most of us, as we get older our priorities do change. We go from being kids who are happy about getting a new toy, to growing older and being happy about the more important priority of having good health.

Some people are so locked into just one area of life that if that doesn't work out well, they feel like they have nothing else. Don't spend all your time trying to empty your life's "in-basket." Almost everyone who tries finds they have neglected all the truly important areas of their life (their faith, family, and friends) in the process.

The most important part of a successful life is having your priorities in order. Because it's these priorities that will carry you to your greatest successes.

If you ever want to see a group of people get

their priorities straight in a hurry, look at the clarity of people who have experienced being in a plane that almost crashed. That really has a way of bringing what is important back into view.

These people are not complaining about the airline meal as they're getting off the plane. They're not feeling sorry for themselves. They're not complaining about the things they don't have in life. Life just gave them a proverbial wake-up call and they lived to tell about it! They are focused on all they have to be thankful for, starting with being alive.

It shouldn't take a near-death experience for us to refocus our view of what is truly important, but for many it does. Take time every day to appreciate and be thankful for your life and the great opportunities you are given. Being thankful is not just a good thing to do, it also happens to be one of the easiest ways to stay positive and focused in life.

If we choose to dwell on negatives, we can find them. But we can just as easily find positives in our lives, if we choose to do so.

Let's face it, we all have problems. But when you are always worried about a seemingly endless array of them, you're not acknowledging the goodness all around you.

Power Principle
"Every problem we encounter has a limited life span, and we control that life span."

It's been proven that most of the things people worry about have either already happened or never will. So why not increase your productive time by focusing on solutions instead of problems? Just remember to focus only on solutions in which you can control the outcome.

Solutions within our control are really opportunities for us to improve our lives because almost all opportunities come to us disguised as problems!

Power Principle
"A problem, like almost everything else, grows when you feed it, so don't grow problems, harvest solutions!"

There's an old joke about the person who

complains about finding a peanut butter and jelly sandwich in their lunch box everyday. A co-worker asks, "Why don't you have your spouse make something else?" The person replies, "I make my own lunch!"

This sounds a little crazy, but it's not all that different from people who complain daily about the way their lives are turning out. They are responsible for where they are and at the same time are doing nothing to change.

If you look in the mirror you *might* see the person who is responsible for making your lunch, but you'll *definitely* see the person most responsible for making or breaking your future.

I'm also reminded of the story about an elderly carpenter who was getting ready to retire. He told his boss with whom he had worked for a very long time, about his plans. He said he would miss the paycheck, but the time had come to retire.

His boss told him he would be sorry to see him leave and asked him if he could build one more house as a favor. The carpenter agreed, but it did not take long to see that his heart wasn't really in his work. His workmanship was uncharacteristically poor and even some of the materials he used were not the best.

On the day of completion, the carpenter's boss came by for inspection. He walked up to the carpenter and handed him the keys to the front door. "This is your house" the boss told the carpenter, "It's my gift to you for all your years of hard work and loyalty."

The carpenter was shocked! He thought, "If I knew I was building my own house, I would have done a better job." Now he had to live with his below-average effort.

This is also true with many of us. We go day by day building our lives with less than our best effort and then are shocked as we look back at what we have created for ourselves. You are the one responsible for the type of future you will construct for yourself. Build wisely!

It's never too late to change your viewpoints in life to align with the right priorities. It's also never too late to be thankful for all that you have, to look at positives and dwell on solutions instead of problems. But you must start now!

Chapter 3

YOUR THOUGHTS CONTROL
YOUR FUTURE

Don't you find it curious that we can say things about ourselves that would makes us furious if they were said by someone else? For instance, you might do something that you think isn't too bright and call yourself an idiot. But if someone else was watching and called you an idiot, you would probably get very upset.

Most people would probably respond to this example by saying, "Well, the difference is, when I say it, I know I'm kidding." The problem is, your subconscious mind doesn't know the difference. It doesn't know kidding from serious; it only processes. Tell yourself "I *can't* do this" and your subconscious begins to process reasons why you are right. Say "I *can* do this" and your mind will again prove you right. That's why Henry Ford's quote, "If you think you can, or if you think you can't, you're right" is so accurate.

Power Principle

"Concern yourself more about what *you* think, than what *others* say."

While we are dealing with state of mind and our subconscious thoughts, I would like to briefly discuss a force called anchoring that is constantly at work shaping our subconscious mind.

Anchoring is something we do most often at high points (when we are happy) or low points (when we are sad) in our lives. Here is an example of what I mean.

Let's say, for example, that someone we know, (let's call him Bob) is attending the funeral of his best friend. I think we can agree this would be an example of a low point in someone's life. As Bob stands and looks at his friend in the casket, someone comes up to him and while putting an arm around him, gives him a little hug and says, "Bob, I'm so sorry, if there is anything I can do, please let me know." This happens almost exactly the same way several times in a row. Bob is now subconsciously anchoring that hug to this event.

30

A year later, with the funeral in the past, Bob is now at a party enjoying himself. Someone who wasn't even at the funeral comes up and gives him that *same* little hug and says, "Hey Bob, how's it going?" Bob instantly becomes saddened and doesn't know why. It is because that hug subconsciously transported him back to the funeral.

Many things have the power to change our state of mind. Have you ever smelled a cake or a pie baking and were immediately transported back to a memory of your mother's or grandmother's kitchen when you were a child?

Have you ever had music change your attitude? An example would be driving down the road, feeling a little depressed, when you reach over and change the radio to a different station that's playing an upbeat song that brings back great memories. Suddenly you joyfully go from driving 20 miles per hour in the right lane to pushing the legal speed limit in the left lane, wondering why everyone doesn't get out of your way.

It can work the other way too. You can be very upbeat and change the radio to a station where you find a song that reminds you of a sad time in your life. Now your perspective changes and you feel that everyone else is driving too fast. It's powerful! And it has to do with anchoring.

I like to play games with it. I know there are certain smells that will always lift my spirit and attitude. Being a kid was an especially happy time for me, so if you see me in an office supply store sniffing a box of crayons, you'll know what's going on.

I have a friend who has also found a way to make anchoring work for him. He started by collecting several different colognes, and whenever he has a very positive experience, he sprays on one of the colognes. What he is doing is anchoring this positive experience to that particular cologne.

Weeks, months or possibly even years later he will be able to recreate the very happy and positive feeling he had when he first used that cologne, simply by spraying it on. The likelihood of this working is affected by a couple of different factors. First, he can't have anchored that cologne previously, even subconsciously. Second, he needs to be linking it to a high point in his life, not just everyday things.

For those of you who might be wrinkling your

nose at this, let me ask you this question. Have you ever detected a certain perfume or cologne and have it immediately remind you of one particular person? Even if that person is someone you have not seen or thought of in years?

Now that you know about anchoring, you can at least be careful with regard to some of the more obvious things being anchored into your subconscious. For instance, it has been proven that the most fertile time to program your mind and anchor positive thoughts is right before you go to bed and right after you wake up.

The problem for many people is, these are times when they watch the news, which for the most part is very negative. Sometimes people who watch the evening news complain they didn't sleep well. That's not too surprising when you look at the images they programmed in right before they went to sleep. If they watch the morning news, they are many times beginning a new day on the wrong foot. Don't get me wrong, I'm not against staying current with events, I'm only advocating the importance of not starting or ending your day with negativity, which unfortunately, the news usually contains.

Many times the first thoughts that enter our minds when we awaken dictate the kind of day we might have. People who have a few things go wrong at the start of a day and comment, "Well, it's going to be one of those days," are setting themselves up to have "one of those days."

The thoughts we choose, either positive or negative, dictate our day. We also get to choose our words, which are just as powerful as our thoughts. For instance, if someone asks you, "How's it going?" and you respond with, "Lousy" or "Not so good" or even the lukewarm "OK, I guess," you are programming your day to be exactly whatever you say.

When you think about it, you could use the words "not bad" and "pretty good" to mean about the same thing. But "pretty good" is more positive and certainly plays better in your subconscious mind.

We can alter our lives and our future simply by altering our thoughts and words. They determine our destination.

Where would you like to be and what would you like to be doing five years from now? Now ask yourself, where do you *really* think you will be and what will you *actually* be doing? Is there a difference between the answers? If so, why?

These questions deal directly with the expectations you have for your future. If what you expect for your future is *lower* than your current status, you are creating a scenario for failure. If what you expect for your future is *equal* to your current status, you are creating a scenario for apathy. But if what you expect for your future is *better* than your current status, you are creating a scenario for motivation!

So if you don't like the direction you are currently heading in life, the single most important thing you can do is to change your thoughts, and with them, your expectations.

Life is like driving a car. Destinations are determined by what is in your mind. Unfortunately, many people drive their "car" of life by always looking in the rear view mirror at what might have been, when they should be looking out the windshield at what could be! Remember, your "car" is powered by your thoughts and it's those thoughts that will determine your destination.

Always remember that any change that can be seen on the outside always starts on the inside first.

To make changes, we must first know where we are. So listen to yourself! Pay close attention to your thoughts, and the things you say to yourself and to others. Become aware of all self-criticism and stop it. Self-criticism serves only one purpose, to program your subconscious mind to fail, which in turn means you will ultimately fail.

Next, feed yourself. To be physically strong you must eat properly and nourish your body with the high-grade fuel it needs. To be mentally strong, you must feed your mind with regular doses of high-grade, positive thoughts.

Power Principle
**"Your mind will grow in direct proportion
to how much you feed it."**

Read or listen to positive messages daily and *reinforce* them throughout the day. You wouldn't starve yourself in an effort to be physically fit, so don't starve your mind of the positive energy it needs to be mentally fit!

This point regarding reinforcement is critical. This is because we are bombarded by negativity and dream stealers on a regular basis. Friends, relatives, news broadcasts, and many of life's other influences have the potential to steal your positive energy. So just like when an army wants to win a battle, you must also bring in constant reinforcements.

It's amazing that there are so many negative people out there when you consider we were *all* born with positive attitudes. All kids talk about what they *want* to be when they grow up, not what they *can't* be.

I heard a story that illustrates how negativity creeps into people's lives starting at an early age. It began with someone going into a first grade classroom and putting a circle on the chalkboard. Then this person asked the children what they thought it was. Some of the answers received were things like, "a spaceship," "a hat," "a ring," "the sun," and of course, "a circle." If you draw the same circle on a chalkboard in a twelfth grade classroom and ask what it represents, the only answer you usually hear is "a circle." All negativity is learned. The good news is it can be unlearned!

If it's true that we usually get out of life what

we expect, why not expect the best? Life is a self-fulfilling prophecy. Your future will usually be what you envision it to be. Expect success and have the proper vision! "See" yourself succeeding before you actually do.

In life, we hit what is pitched. But most times we can *dictate* what will be pitched by expecting and envisioning the best for ourselves.

Expect the best for yourself and your family. Get into the habit of programming positive thoughts and images throughout the day, every day.

Power Principle
"Positive thinking is perceiving. Positive believing is the beginning of achieving."

There is tremendous power in believing. Start each day by programming the outcome in advance. You do this by simply envisioning positive thoughts for a positive outcome. Envision your way to a perfect day, evening, career, relationship and life. Don't take this lightly and the rewards can be plentiful!

Remember, the mind only holds one thought at

a time, so focus it on the positive ones. Turn all negative thoughts into positive ones immediately. Don't let negative thoughts linger.

Professional athletes do this every day. Quarterbacks expect to complete passes, not throw interceptions. Race car drivers expect to turn fast laps, not hit walls. Professional athletes wouldn't last very long if they focused on failure. Ever hear a boxer in a pre-fight interview say he can't win? Hardly, but we hear co-workers and associates say it every day! We are also in a fight everyday, a fight to succeed. But just like the athlete, without the right attitude we don't stand a chance. Always focus on success, not failure!

Power Principle
"When will it hit you that you have always possessed the power to succeed?"

Check your attitude and thoughts throughout the day, as you would look at a road map while on a trip. It's easy to drift when you consider all the negativity that surrounds us on a daily basis.

Each day is really part of a lifelong journey,

with each step taking us closer to, or farther away from, our ultimate goals in life. Checking your thoughts and direction is critical to staying on course, because...

Power Principle
"All thoughts, whether positive or negative, grow stronger with repetition."

Too many people spend too much time complaining about bad breaks and what others have done to them.

Power Principle
"Spend time trying to prove to others what your problems and limitations are and you will own those problems and limitations."

Anytime you want to look at the person who has the potential to do you the most good or harm, just look in the mirror!

The choices we make everyday determine the type of lives we will have. It's like adjusting the lens on a camera. The constant adjustments you make as well as what you focus on determine what you will "see" in our life. Always "picture" a wonderful and positive future and you will have one!

Chapter 4

PROTECTING YOUR ENVIRONMENT

When two fighters enter the ring for a boxing match, one of the last instructions they receive from the referee is, "Protect yourself at all times." Not bad advice. And not just for the fighters, but for us in our everyday lives, too.

Protecting yourself involves many facets. To start with, having all the wonderful things in life is meaningless without your health. Guard your health as you would a pile of gold, because that's how valuable it is. In fact, I believe it is even more valuable than gold. If we are fortunate enough to have our health, we are all worth millions.

Don't believe me? Let me ask you a question. It would probably be pretty easy to find a hospital in which an extremely wealthy person is terminally ill. If there was a way for that person to give you all of his or her millions in return for the ability to have your good health, do you think they would offer it? Would you accept?

Whenever I ask anyone this question the response I most often hear is, "I never looked at it that way before."

Almost everyone who says that does so because they have been blessed with at least relatively good health. As a result they have taken it for granted.

I remember a time a number of years ago when I was injured playing basketball and wound up on crutches for nearly three months. The frustration of stumbling around on crutches to do even the simplest of things really got to me. Suffice it to say, after that I no longer took walking for granted.

Too many people wait until they become ill to begin paying attention to their health. Practice preventative maintenance. Read books on proper nutrition and speak with nutritional experts. Do something positive for good health everyday. Work on it as if your life depended on it, because it does!

I also need to make a quick mention of stress. It is one of the top killers in our country. That's amazing when you realize that we produce our own stress. It is almost never what happens to you, but how you react to it, that matters! What things mean to us are governed by the perceptions *we* attach to them. Things are only as good or as bad as *we* perceive!

We are in total control of the amount of stress we place on ourselves in any given situation. For example, waiting in line has an entirely different feel to it when you are pressed for time, versus when you have no other particular place to go.

Stress can take years off your life. Keep that in mind the next time someone cuts you off in traffic. Situations are constantly changing in our lives, but we are the ones who get to choose how we will react. Why not look at them as an opportunity to practice your sense of humor?

Of course, protecting your environment involves more than protecting your health. It also means protecting your immediate surroundings, because it is these surroundings that help dictate your future. In every area of your life, the choices you make today determine who and what you will become tomorrow. Don't be careless with these choices!

One area in which choices are critical is the building of your success team. None of us knows everything, so it's important to surround ourselves with the most effective team possible. It's the best team that is usually the most successful in sports, and so it is with life.

At some point, you will probably need an attorney, tax accountant and a financial adviser. Do not rush through these choices! There are good and bad in every profession. Get the best person, or at least someone very good. If you were sick, you would want the best doctor because it could mean your life. It's the same with your financial and business health. Seek out the leaders in your industry and learn who they are using and why.

There can be a large difference between people who graduate at the top of their class and those who graduate at the bottom, but the titles these people carry remain the same. An accountant is still an accountant, a lawyer is still a lawyer, but the level of knowledge can differ dramatically. Even someone who graduates with the lowest grades in their class in medical school is still called a doctor! Get good people around you. Your future depends on it. Another area in which it is important to be diligent is when choosing friends. Choose people who are compatible with your goals. This will help you to motivate each other toward success.

It also ties in to a critically important success principle stated by motivational speaker and best selling author, Zig Ziglar. "You can have everything in life you want if you will just help enough other people get what they want."

Birds of a feather really do flock together, so choose your friends carefully. I read somewhere that most people's annual income equals the average income of their five closest friends. This tells me two things. One, our choices can make dramatic differences in our lives, and two, we should all be hanging out with rich people!

Power Principle
"Constant personal development is critical. Make a commitment to do something everyday to improve yourself. There is no good alternative to growing!"

We definitely need to avoid those who belittle or berate our dreams and ambitions. It's better to be by yourself than to associate with people who are negative or want nothing more than to steal your dreams. No one erects statues of great "negative" thinkers.

Here's an idea you can try to get the negativity out of meetings and gatherings. Place a bowl on the table and tell everyone that with every negative comment, the perpetrator has to kick in one dollar. If someone says that's a stupid idea, thank that person for getting the fund started.

Negativism is nothing more than a great repellent. It repels positive people, along with a wonderful and bright future for yourself and your family. If you saw someone holding a sign that read, "I'm negative. I can't and won't succeed! I'm also going to try to get you to think that way too," would you befriend that person? Just because negative people don't carry signs makes them no less dangerous to your progress and your future.

If you were a landlord, you wouldn't let a tenant rent an apartment from you while allowing them to ruin your building. So why let negative people rent space in your mind and ruin your thoughts? Never let others control your attitude or thoughts. Remember, choose your friends wisely, as they will impact your future.

It is always easier to be enthusiastic when the people around you are that way too. Enthusiasm is contagious, if you have it, share it!

I have always believed the greatest gift you can give someone is the gift of encouragement. I think this is even truer when we realize the average child today hears the word "no" about 140,000 times by the time he or she turns eighteen.

An important part of protecting your environment is taking time to enjoy it. The road to success has many twists and turns. It also has many places to pull over and rest. Naturally, resting is OK as long as the rest stops don't become permanent parking places!

Take time every day to appreciate all the wonderful possessions in your life. Think of one particular thing every day for which you are grateful. I tend to start with the physical items, such as eyesight, hearing, and my overall health. If you are fortunate enough to be relatively healthy and don't take time to be thankful for it every day, you are missing the big picture. There are also other things to be thankful for such as a nice home, your family and your friends. Construct your own list and see how long you can make it!

The subject of gratitude reminds me of a couple of thought-provoking analogies. The first is for everyone who takes things they have for granted. Imagine for a moment that all of your personal possessions are about to be lost in a fire. Now imagine you are given the opportunity to salvage only *one* of these possessions and you have only a few moments to decide which item you want to save. What would it be? Do you wish you could save more than one item? Of course you do! You have probably spent a lifetime building up everything you have.

Now imagine that the fire suddenly stopped and that everything was safe. How would you feel? Grateful? Good news! Because that's where you are right now. You have everything right at this very moment. Appreciate it!

Power Principle

"Always be thankful for what you have, not disappointed over things you don't have."

The second analogy is for the people who wish they were someone else. They see athletes or movie stars and wish their lives were like theirs. Imagine this. You are given one opportunity to be tossed back into the "barrel of life," meaning you would be tossed around and could come out as anyone, anywhere in the world.

You might emerge as the most attractive person or maybe the wealthiest. You might also come out as someone in an underdeveloped nation who is battling disease and poverty. Would you take this chance? Virtually everyone I share this analogy with says, "No way!" The reason is, even though they would like to be someone else, their own lives are too good to risk trading for the possibility of something far worse. In other words, do you think you are better or worse off than most others?

The point is that it's important to take the time to think and reflect. Be thankful and appreciate all that you currently have. Be comfortable with who you are. Enjoying the journey is as important as reaching the destination. Don't miss the scenery!

Chapter 5

GO FOR THE GOALS!

You might be saying to yourself, "Gee, Dave, a goal setting chapter in a motivational book, I'm shocked!" I know, it seems like almost every self-help book has some mention of goal setting, and for good reason. It's because setting goals is one of the most effective ways to create a successful life! The odd part is that almost everyone knows this, yet few people have taken the time to write out clear and concise goals.

Almost anyone would tell you that his or her future is more important than any two-week vacation. Most people go on vacation with a plan, road maps and a carefully thought out destination. Ironically, many of these same people will go through the rest of their lives without any of these things!

Power Principle
**"If you don't have a plan for success,
you already have a plan for failure."**

See if this sounds familiar. I was having a conversation with a good friend of mine one afternoon when he said, "You know, I didn't seem to get a thing accomplished today." So I asked him, "What did you have written down on your 'to-do' list today?" He said, "Nothing." So I replied, "Congratulations! You accomplished everything you set out to do!"

People without goals are like ships without rudders, directionless. And just like those ships, they will get pushed in many directions, never getting to their true destinations.

When was the last time you started looking for something but didn't know what it was or where to begin looking for it? You might say, "That's crazy, no one does that." But, have you ever talked with people who wanted to be successful, but didn't even know what their definitions of success were? They are searching for something that they themselves have yet to define. See the irony? You must have a plan. Even a mediocre plan is better than no plan at all.

At this point I would like to ask you the following question: What is your number one goal in life? If you have to think about it, you don't have one.

The reason I say that is, a true number one goal should always be forefront in your mind. In other words, it doesn't matter when someone asks, you have the answer. Whether it's right now as you read this book, or even at 3 o'clock in the morning, the answer is the same. (Although, I will admit if you have someone asking you what your number one goal in life is at 3 a.m., you might have bigger concerns than remembering your goals!)

Power Principle
"You can make progress or you can make excuses, but not both."

I have heard all the excuses when it comes to reasons why people don't set goals. There are people who say, "I just can't seem to set goals and stick to them." My response is, "Could you do it if someone paid you $2,000 per day?" If the answer is yes, then we have isolated the problem. It's not a lack of ability, but a lack of commitment! Then there are those who admit they don't have dreams or goals because they don't want to be disappointed. The reality is, they are the ones who will be the most disappointed. Another common excuse is, "I just seem to be too tired at the end the day to go through a goal setting exercise." The truth is many times when people believe they are too tired, it's only because they don't have anything stimulating their minds.

It's always easy to find the energy when it involves something we truly want to do. So find something to get excited about, something you really believe in and want to do. Find a cause to champion or a career path you want to follow, and be sure it's something you can get excited about.

Power Principle
"Excite your mind toward goals you believe in and your body will follow!"

No goal-setting chapter would be complete without the requisite goal setting list. I believe every chapter in this book is important, but without a strategy to implement your ideas, plans and goals, you are wasting your time! So without further ado: Goal Setting 101.

1.) <u>Dream big!</u>

First, dreams are free. Second, they're fun! If you had a magic wand, what would you wish for? Or just ask yourself, "What would I try if I knew I could not fail?" And wait for the answer. Don't rush this, the answer is critical. Then ask yourself, "What's stopping me?" Remember, excite the mind and the body will follow.

<u>Power Principle</u>
"With every dream you are also given the power to make it come true."

You are the architect and builder of your future. You choose the plans and blueprints you want to follow. Don't build walls that keep you from your dreams, build roads that will take you there.

<u>Power Principle</u>
"People can only be as great as their dreams and goals allow them to be."

2.) *Fine-tune your dreams!*

Focus! It's one of the secrets to a successful life. Unless we are able to focus on the particular goals we want to attain, they become just wishes and nearly impossible to reach. For example, a magnifying glass does nothing if you merely wave it around, but it can burn through objects on which it is focused. Successful people may be able to do several things well, but it's their ability to focus that enables them to succeed.

These people are like laser beams, not strobe lights. A strobe light flashes on and off, going in many directions at once. You don't think of power and precision. You think of something that is fun to watch but doesn't accomplish much.

The people who are the "strobe lights" in life are the same way. Sometimes they're "on" and sometimes they aren't. They're usually going in many directions at once and find it difficult to get anything accomplished. The people who are the "laser beams" in life are the ones that have power and precision. Their power comes from the ability to concentrate on the goals and tasks at hand. Their precision is created by focusing their energy toward these tasks.

Always focus on what you want. Too many people know what they *don't* want, and that's what they incorrectly focus on.

By focusing, you will be able to fine-tune and achieve *exactly* what you want. How can you attain any thought or dream if you don't know *exactly* what it is? For instance, let's assume a dream of yours is to be in business for yourself. Now, fine-tune it! What kind of business do you want? Do you want to have employees or associates? Do you want to work from home or from a storefront? Continue the fine-tuning by making these dreams as measurable as possible.

Making goals measurable is the only way to see if progress is being made. For instance, if you are leading an organization and one of your goals is to become a better leader, fine. But make it measurable by taking certain leadership courses, or by making a point of studying a specific number of others inside or outside your organization who possess great leadership capabilities. Another idea might be to commit to reading one book a month written by a great leader.

3.) Go to the movies!

What? Well, I could have written that you

should start envisioning your dreams happening, but that would have been boring! By going to the movies, I mean you should start seeing these finely tuned dreams in your mind, playing them over and over again like a movie. And since you are the director, you can select the outcome! To help you "see" this movie, place copies of the "script" around where you will see them. Post-it notes, pictures, or whatever it takes to keep these dreams foremost in your mind.

Power Principle
"You are halfway to any goal if you can
first see yourself achieving it!"

4.) Have a passionate conviction toward
achieving your dreams!

I can't overstate this one. You must be passionate about achieving what you want in life. When your passion drops, your results drop exponentially. Passion toward what you want will drive you, and conviction in your beliefs will sustain you.

What level of conviction am I referring to? I'll give you an example. If I ask you, "How much is two plus two?" You would probably say, "Four." And you would probably be pretty sure of that. So sure in fact, that if I tried to make an argument for the correct answer really being five, no matter what I said I would be unable to shake you from your answer.

It's that level of conviction and belief you must have in your own dreams and goals! This unshakeable conviction is a must because people will always try to tell you that you're wrong or that you should give up trying to achieve the things you really want in life.

Power Principle
"Dreams turn into mere wishes without conviction. Success goes to those with a burning desire to succeed, not to those with only a passing interest in success."

5.) *Make sure your goals are attainable.*

Unshakeable conviction can obviously only come from dreams and goals we *know* we can attain. I believe a positive attitude is very important because I think people can do anything *they* believe is possible! Of course a positive attitude alone is not enough.

There are many things I know I can do, but even if I was the most positive-minded person on the face of the earth, there is still no chance I could become the heavyweight champion of the world. This is not an attainable goal for me. First, I only weigh 175 pounds, and second, I don't like people hitting me. Only when you know your goals are attainable, can you build the unshakeable conviction you will need to attain them.

Power Principle
**"We achieve only what we
perceive and truly believe."**

6.) _Set a definite time period to achieve your goals._

Having dreams and setting goals is great, but it is only half the job. You must also set a definite time frame in which to achieve them. If you master only half the job of setting goals, but not setting time frames, your chances for success are greatly diminished.

7.) _Commit your goals to writing._

This is one of the most important steps in the entire process. Many studies have examined what makes people successful. Time after time, the common denominator was not just having goals, but committing them to writing.

I remember reading about one particular study that was conducted with graduating seniors at a major university. Only three-percent had specific goals that were written down. Twenty years later, this same class was surveyed again and it was found that the three-percent who had written down goals had outperformed the other ninety-seven-percent combined! It only makes sense to write our goals down, but here again, only a small percentage of the population actually does it.

Think of a time when you were lost and asked someone for directions. (I am probably speaking mostly to the women readers, since most men never ask for directions when they are lost!) If someone tells you to, "Go two blocks, make a left, then go about one mile to the second traffic light where you will make a right, then pass the small convenience store, which is about a half-mile down the road, then make two quick lefts." Would you more likely to get there if you write the directions down on paper?

Well, it's the same with your dreams and goals.

Remember, having goals without putting them in writing is like not having goals at all.

8.) *Take action!*

To use the last example, if you had the right directions but didn't start the car, you would never reach your destination. This may seem obvious but many people are stricken with a dangerous, yet very curable disease, known as "analysis paralysis." People stricken with this disease will usually do the first seven steps listed here, but will over-analyze them to the degree that they never take action, usually because they are afraid to make a mistake.

Power Principle
"The biggest mistake anyone can make is to be afraid of making one."

Don't forget to check and re-check your goals every six months, always being watchful to see if they are taking you closer to or further away from your ultimate objectives.

After all, being motivated and having a positive attitude are only part of the winning picture. Proper direction in life is equally important. Your goals are your compass in life. Make sure they are constantly pointing you in the right direction.

Mastering the game of golf means getting the distance *and* direction correct on every shot. You won't be very successful if you have the right distance and the wrong direction, or vice versa.

It's the same with your dreams and goals. If you are very motivated without a goal strategy, you've got the distance part right, but your direction will probably be off.

Many people in the last days of their lives have admitted to wishing they had lived their lives differently. Don't let that happen to you! Have a plan for your life every day. Know where you want to be in one year, in five years, in ten years and beyond.

If you don't make your own choices, they will be made for you. Define your life, or it will define you. And the best way to define your life is through proper goal setting.

Power Principle
**"Live every day as if it were your last,
but plan as if you will live forever!"**

Chapter 6

IT'S ABOUT TIME!

Whenever I ask someone, "If a magic genie could grant you three wishes, what would they be?" I hear many of the same responses. The most frequent response usually has something to do with receiving large quantities of money. I can't remember anyone asking the "magic genie" for more time.

Yet, time is the most valuable commodity we have. Without it, not much else matters. In spite of this, most people pay little attention to what they do with it and how they trade it everyday.

My view of time is that when you're born, a checking account is opened in your name and a single deposit is made. That deposit is not made with money or gold, it's more valuable than both combined. It's the most valuable commodity of all, time.

Your time account is quite a bit different than a regular checking account. First, that original deposit will be the only deposit ever made for the duration of your life. And, unlike a regular checking account, you must draw on your time account constantly, whether you want to or not. Another difference is that you will never be told the balance in your time account. You must keep drawing on it every day until suddenly you are informed the balance is zero and the account is closed.

Lastly, unlike your cash account, there are no refunds on your time account. If you don't like what you received for the time you traded, too bad.

Power Principle
"Time is the most important currency we have.
Don't trade it for things that can't
help you reach your goals."

Money can be invested to make more money. But even though time can be "invested wisely," it never creates more time. We can't do anything to add more time to our account. We exchange it everyday at the same exact rate, 24 hours.

One thing time and money have in common is the more you have of either, the less valuable they seem to be.

When you are young, there seems to be an endless supply of time. But it can be an illusion, because no one can guarantee that tomorrow is scheduled. I'm sure many of us can remember sitting in school wishing time would "hurry up." I'm also fairly sure you're no longer asking for that same wish. That's because you have aged, using up a portion of your account while seeing other people's accounts closed out entirely. This has a tendency to make you want to evaluate some of the choices you have made.

So the next time a pilot announces, "We're a little behind schedule, so we're going to have to 'make up' time," or if a friend says, "I guess I am just going to have to 'find more time' to get these things done," get them to show you how they plan to do it. (If they ever do find a way, please call me immediately!) Although we can't create more time, what we can do is rearrange our schedules to make better use of the time we have.

For instance, let's say someone we know would like to get involved in a part-time business. But at the moment there is a struggle going on as to how this person will spend his or her "time credits." Start a new business, or watch television? It's so easy to think, "I

69

always wanted to be in business for myself, but this is a really good TV night!" Meanwhile, the clock continues to run.

Don't get me wrong. Watching TV is fine. We all have to have fun, and if that is your type of fun, great. What I'm saying is, if you fast-forward your life in your mind, will you look back at all the TV you watched and say it was a great exchange of your time, or will you wish you had done something else?

There are numerous similarities between life and sports. Competition, teamwork, as well as winning and losing are a few examples. But at least one big difference would have to be that in life, there are no "time-outs." (Although you parents may have children who disagree with this.) A time-out for grownups would be great. We could stop the clock. (Please understand it's also my intention that you would be able to restart it!) We could take a time-out when things get tough, or when we need a break or have a big decision to make. But instead the clock always runs, constantly demanding that we manage time properly to make the most out of it.

I have played chess most of my life. Contrary to

popular belief, tournament games are not comprised of two people sitting at a board taking whatever amount of time they want to make their moves. A chess clock is always used, and if no one has won "on the board," the first player to run out of time loses.

Many times players who are in "time trouble" (about to run out of time) are forced into making bad moves because they don't have as much time to think as they would like. For that reason, many times the winner of a chess game is the person who made the best use of their time. It's not all that different from life!

For some people, time is a mystery. They walk around saying things like, "I don't know where the time went." Well, it was exchanged for something else. All of us used up 24 hours yesterday, as we have every day prior to that. We exchange time for working, eating, bathing, watching TV, or any number of other things. We exchange it for what we believe is important.

Power Principle
"To manage time better we must set priorities. Because those who try to make everything a priority will succeed in making nothing a priority."

So how can we make better use of our time? I believe to do that, we must first track what we are exchanging it for now.

So start by taking a four-week period and keeping a record of what you are exchanging your time for on an hourly basis. Don't do anything differently than you are doing now. You will be amazed at how much time is wasted every day. From this you can determine where changes need to be made, and then you can implement your new schedule.

Begin planning your day, every day, with schedules and follow them. Draw up "must do" lists and carry them with you. Here are some other ideas to better manage your time:

1.) _Avoid people who just want to "shoot the breeze."_

You know the ones. The "coffee clutchers" who are always seen clutching their coffee with the sole purpose of getting you to stop and have a cup with them. The "water buffaloes" are perpetrators of the same time-wasting tactics as the "coffee clutchers," except they are usually found near the water cooler. All they will help you do is mismanage your time.

2.) Stop worrying about every little thing in your life.

Worry time is wasted time. Studies have shown that many of the things people worry about have either already happened or never will.

3.) Stop procrastinating!

Procrastination is the thief of time. Everyone has something they have been putting off doing. Do at least one thing that you have been putting off doing, and do it *today*!

4.) Be where you are.

I remember one particular instance when I was at an important seminar. Since it was rather costly, I was taking copious notes. On the first break, I called my office to see if I had any messages. My assistant told me one of my top associates called in and was quite upset about something. She told me he was so upset she couldn't even make out what the problem was. She said, "You'd better call him immediately." I did. He was out.

The seminar began again and now I'm not taking any notes. My mind was on that associate and what he could possibly be that upset about. The entire afternoon went by with my mind focused somewhere else.

When I returned to the office, I found that he had called again and left a message that read, "Ignore that earlier message, I got everything worked out. Sorry for the misunderstanding." I got all worked up over nothing and there was nothing more I could have done during the seminar anyway. So because my focus was elsewhere, I ended up wasting my time and my money.

The point is, if you are physically in one place, but mentally somewhere else, it's purely just a bad exchange of your time. The money I spent for the seminar I will earn again, but I can never regain the time. Always be where you are!

One way to determine if you are doing what you really want with your life is to pay attention to how often your mind and body are in the same place.

If you are just "going through the motions" then resolve today to start managing your time more wisely and going after what you really want in life.

Remember, time is our most precious commodity! You trade a part of your life every day for that which you believe is important. Make sure that it is! Control the time you are given or it will control you!

Chapter 7

UNLOCKING THE POWER

As I grew up I was conditioned by the status quo. The way to be successful was to get a good job, work 30 or more years and collect a pension when you retired. In fact when I was young and landed my first "good job" I looked around and saw people working for themselves and wondered how they could work every day without the security offered by a large corporation. That security was a reality back then. But not any more!

Anyway, back to my first "good job." I would soon find out that lack of security was only one problem I would encounter while working in the corporate world. I would also find out that "job" was an acronym for "just over broke."

I had lunch with a self-employed friend one day and he asked me, "How's everything in prison?" I looked at him and said, "What?" He replied, "Well, that's not entirely accurate, I guess. Your cubicle *is* actually smaller than a prisoner's cell. And you don't get your own toilet, you have to share with everyone on your floor. Oh, and prisoners are allowed to make personal calls, aren't they?" He made his point. Well, I might have been in prison, but the door was locked from the inside and I had the key.

After 16 years and two promotions, I took a step back and saw some amazing things. All of a sudden it seemed as if the building I worked in was shaped like a pyramid. Figuratively, not literally, of course. What I mean is, everyone who worked there started at the bottom. And we were all working to reach the top. Now if there were unlimited positions open at the top, this would have been fine. But there weren't. So we were all working toward attaining an extremely limited number of top positions. This created a pyramid few would ever actually scale.

We all know that even if you are able to move up, it becomes exponentially harder the higher you go. Your supervisor is partially to blame for this. He or she doesn't want you passing them up, or even worse, getting their job. That's why you are held down with whatever methods are available to them. These could include unflattering reviews, being excluded from new training classes, or just being left out of the loop entirely. If you are fortunate enough to move up, you don't usually go straight up, you move up a little and hit a plateau.

Here is where the picture changed for me again. I had been promoted twice and was now standing on a nice comfortable plateau. I began looking to move up again, but that's when I noticed something I hadn't seen before. I had shackles on each leg with a tag on each one. One read, "No four year college degree," and another read, "Turned down transfer." They could have also read, "Not very good at playing politics."

These shackles were holding me back from further advancement. I started realizing that just trying hard and being good at my job wasn't going to be good enough. I got tired of seeing others pass me by because of "who they knew."

I also noticed something else. That plateau I was standing on was turning into a ledge. Because I was getting older, and my chances of moving up were fading, I was becoming more expendable. I was beginning to experience a form of "desk rage." It was the internal kind (no firearms were involved). I thought to myself, "I'm tired of building someone else's dream."

77

Freedom is the most precious gift we have and I began to realize that I wasn't really free at all. The corporation had built a box around me. The floor and ceiling of the box were the minimum and maximum they would pay me for my position and the side walls were the benefits that kept me in the box. This "income box" is a reality for almost every job, regardless of level.

Being paid a salary is analogous to a teacher telling a room full of students that from today on, everyone in the class will make a C, meaning there will no longer be any A's or B's, D's or F's.

What this does is punish the A and B students, while rewarding the D and F students. Just like a salary pays for a position, regardless of the ability of the person holding that position.

My salary dictated the kind of house I lived in, the type of car I drove, as well as where I went on vacation.

As I started to see the clear picture, I began to not care much for my "career." Don't get me wrong. It was a really good job if you only had a short time to live, because every day seemed like a lifetime.

This chapter is near and dear to me because it was not easy for me to decide the corporate world wasn't for me, especially because it was all I knew up to that point in my life.

But leaving the corporate world is a goal shared by many. As I speak with people everywhere, I find a large number of people dreaming of owning their own businesses and being their own bosses.

One thing I learned is, if you don't change, neither will your future. If you hate Mondays something is wrong. If Wednesday is hump day to you, something is wrong. If you refer to every Friday as T.G.I.F., something is wrong. Everyday on earth is a precious gift. You should be living it, not enduring it!

Power Principle
"Turn your vocation into a vacation and you will never have to "work" again."

Let's face it, when you are doing what you love, it's not work. We can get caught up for hours doing something we love and wonder where the time went. That is how you can identify a true entrepreneur –

someone who would rather work 16 hours a day for themselves than 8 hours a day for someone else.

I began looking for what I considered to be the "perfect" business for me. Following are the issues I addressed as I went about selecting this business.

1.) The ability to start part time.

I do not advocate you quitting your job until your new business is going well. This is because it usually adds too much pressure to walk away from something that is paying the bills when your venture is new. This is especially true if you have a family to support. My feeling is that you should not leave your job until after your part-time income equals your full-time income.

2.) No large investment (start up capital) required.

With most of today's big name franchises requiring thousands, if not hundreds of thousands or in some cases millions of dollars to launch, finding a business you can start for only a small investment is ideal. This is an important requirement because when most people start out, a small investment is the only kind they can afford to make. Having a business that allows you to work out of your home can help to cut overhead expenses. A home-based business also allows many people to spend more time with their families.

3.) *No employees.*

My experience has been, that from the standpoint of paperwork alone, working with independent contractors is preferable to working with employees.

4.) *Worldwide and unrestricted market.*

One of the most important things you need to grow your business big is the ability to market your products anywhere. You should have as close to a worldwide market for your products and/or services as possible. And, so that you don't trade a job with shackles for a career with shackles, make sure your market is unrestricted. This means you will not have any particular territory to which you will be confined.

5.) *Great products.*

This seems obvious, but there are a number of reasons why this is important. First, great products are highly marketable, not just to the public, but to you. I mention this because I know people who don't use the very products they market. I don't know about you, but

I've never really been able to market anything I didn't truly believe in. Having great products to market solves this problem. Also, the products you represent should be able to help others by making a significant contribution to their lives.

6.) Unlimited and residual income.

Find an opportunity in which the person is paid, not the position, and any advancement and income is based solely on your effort. Build your organization so that it takes on a life of its own while you're being paid over and over for very little extra effort.

7.) Easy to reproduce system.

Be in business *for* yourself, not *by* yourself. Since success always leaves clues, why re-invent the wheel? There are already systems in place that have worked for others, why not just copy them?

Your new business should meet all of the above criteria, not three or four out of seven -- all seven. Just as with a jigsaw puzzle, the clearest picture comes only when all the pieces are in place.

One of my products is an investment-related cassette tape, titled *Grow Your Own Money Tree!* On it I explain that one of the steps to building wealth is practicing ownership instead of "loanership." This is a message that also fits here. It's much better to own your own business than to practice "loanership" by building someone else's business.

We all know there are no guarantees in life. For me, however, the road to having my own business and becoming my own boss was harder than I thought it would be, but more worthwhile than I could ever have imagined.

Chapter 8

THE LOST ART OF LEADERSHIP

Lead, follow, or get out of the way. My dad always used to say the person who didn't lead or follow made a great roadblock.

It seems to me that "real" leadership is more important today than ever before. And not just leadership, but quality leadership. This applies to the people upline as well as downline in any organization. By quality leadership, I'm talking about respecting and keeping everybody in both your upline and downline informed. Business today is a battle and you cannot manage your people into battle, you must *lead* them!

Power Principle
"If you want to get the best out of people, look for the best in them first."

Leaders know that failure is only a temporary setback, not a final stopping point. Leaders know how to get back on track and how to help others do the same. Leaders fail without fear, and help others do the same because they know it is a step in the journey to success!

A leader must have thick skin, because he or she is the one out front. Leaders know that if you aren't the lead dog, the view never changes. Taking the lead often means taking the most criticism, and a true leader is ready for that. Leaders know they must stay fired up when others try to extinguish their flames.

Real leadership is a rare quality today. What you *say* as a leader is important, but what you *do* is even more important.

Power Principle
"Your actions speak so loudly,
people don't hear what you are saying."

Having the respect of others is critical to being a leader. Since respect cannot be purchased for any price, it must be earned. I have always believed the best way to earn the respect of others is to first develop self-respect, then give your respect to those who are deserving. And again, always remember to lead by doing!

Power Principle

**"People can't lead *you* where *they* haven't been
and *you* can't lead *others* where you have not
gone or are unwilling to go."**

Many years ago I wanted to buy my first home.
I only had one problem. I didn't have much money. As
problems go, this could have been a big one. I had
heard of people buying homes for "nothing down,"
which is a method of buying without a down payment. I
knew I needed help from someone who had already
been successful in this area. After all, how much
confidence would you have in someone helping you
who had never bought a home this way themselves?
When I found someone who was an expert in these
transactions, I bought my first home with only $855 in
out-of-pocket expenses.

You can find examples of people trying to lead
where they haven't been themselves virtually
everywhere. My first experience with this came in my
personal finance class in college. Our teacher admitted
to the class on the very first day that he had never
achieved any real personal wealth himself, but that he

87

was excited about teaching this class. I felt an emotion too, but it wasn't excitement. I sat there and listened to the teacher basically tell us, "I never figured out how to handle my own finances in a way that created financial security for myself, but I'm excited about sharing what I know with all of you."

This opened my eyes. Over time I realized this problem was not confined to personal finance class. Did you ever have a wood shop teacher who had missing fingers? Or how about a physical education teacher who was overweight? See what I mean? And it doesn't stop there. Did you ever meet a financial adviser who was, for all intents and purposes, broke? Or couldn't balance his or her own checkbook?

Just because someone has a title or a degree doesn't guarantee he or she knows the subject well enough to lead!

Let me explain my reason for touching on the subject of the "unleader." It's because we are not born knowing everything, so by necessity we are all followers at one time or another. Therefore it's critical that the people we choose to follow have actually accomplished the things we want to accomplish.

Seek out those who can help you. After all, there are really only two forms of knowledge. The knowledge you have and the knowledge of others, found through relationships, books, tapes, and other means. When you need to accomplish something, don't reinvent the wheel. Seek out those who have already accomplished what you want in life. Save time learning from the experience of others.

Be aware, however, that the road to success has many twists and turns. Almost everyone is willing to give you their version of a road map. Make sure you only consider following maps from those who have actually made the trip successfully! Be sure you are following a leader, not a follower who is looking for a leader.

Now that we have covered that, let's get back to leaders. Real leaders made this country great and continue to do so. You show me any successful business, network marketing company, church or charitable group, and I will show you an organization run by a leader!

Following is a list of the outstanding qualities that I believe make someone a leader:

1.) Leaders exhibit loyalty.

This doesn't mean they always agree with everything everyone says, but whenever they question something, they always do it with the best intentions. This loyalty expands in both directions. It extends to the people they are working under and also to those working under them.

2.) Leaders are courageous.

They're not afraid to fail and they don't run from challenges. They don't let obstacles and barriers stop them from reaching their goals.

3.) Leaders are tenacious.

They have the ability to continue to push on when roadblocks appear. Anyone can prosper when things are going well. But even with the most positive of attitudes, there will be times when things don't go smoothly.

Leaders have the mental stamina to fight through the rough times, and are unwilling to yield to the barriers that stand in their way. Leaders always appreciate what they have but are never satisfied. They know they are not perfect and work every day to improve.

4.) *Leaders are confident and decisive.*

Leaders don't keep changing their minds on the issues pertaining to running their organizations. All that does is breed doubt and concern.

They understand the important correlation between confidence and leadership. This means sounding, looking, and acting confidently.

An example of sounding confident would be the response you would have if someone asked you to get something done by the end of the week that you knew would not be hard to do. You wouldn't respond with, "I think I can get that accomplished," or "I'll try." You would respond with, "I'm sure I'll have that completed on time." Not speaking confidently inwardly affects your subconscious and outwardly affects your team.

Looking confident means paying attention to your appearance. Dress well and look sharp! This affects the subconscious because we always feel better about ourselves when we look our best.

Acting confident refers to our body language. Stand up straight, keep your head up and shoulders back. Your mental state is better when your posture is better. It becomes more difficult to be depressed when your body language is correct.

5.) Leaders are accountable.

They do not lay the blame for their failures on someone else. They are always accountable for their own actions and hold others accountable for their actions.

6.) Leaders are responsible.

They hold themselves to a high standard of ethics. They can always be counted on to do what is right and fair. They treat everyone equally and don't play favorites.

7.) Leaders are dependable.

They finish projects on time and return calls in a timely manner. In short, they do what they say they're going to do. Being dependable covers many areas. Simply put, if you promise to return someone's call, do it. If you promise to meet someone somewhere, do it. Whenever you promise something to someone, always follow through. Build a reputation as someone who can always be counted on.

8.) Leaders are always "up."

Let me clarify. We all have times when we are not at our best or when we feel a little down or depressed. And that's OK as long as you don't let others in your organization see you that way. Of course, you must also make the effort to turn your thoughts around to thinking positively again.

Power Principle
"Don't tell people your problems, 80% don't care and 20% are glad you have them."

I believe a leader has to have all of the eight preceding qualities because people will not follow or believe in a disillusioned, whining crybaby. Leaders have to look like leaders, act like leaders and handle their business affairs and organizations like leaders. Leaders never ask anyone to do anything they would not do themselves. No job is too big or too small. Show me someone who can't find the time to do the small things in life and I'll show you someone who probably can't be trusted to do the big things.

Leaders don't nag or belittle their people to get results, they encourage them. They know how to make them feel special.

They share their enthusiasm and develop other

93

leaders through *genuine* encouragement. Leaders never praise themselves and always praise others in public when the praise has been earned.

Power Principle
"Expect the best out of others or expect to receive mediocrity."

Praise is powerful. The best present you can give someone is the gift of encouragement. Remember, to give is important. To give when it is not expected is even more important.

One of the best ways to be a leader in your organization is through the use of sincere praise. *Sincere is* the key word. There is almost nothing worst than feint praise. It fools no one and does nothing but damage to an organization.

Sincere praise can lift people. When it comes from the heart it actually has a two-pronged effect. It helps both the person receiving it and the person giving it. Offer someone sincere, heartfelt praise for something they have accomplished and see if it doesn't lift you too.

94

My first lesson with the power of praise outside the home came in the seventh grade in science class. It happened during the first year that students changed classes and teachers every hour instead of having the same teacher for all subjects.

When I walked into the science class I noticed 10 chairs separated from the other 25 chairs in the room. I, of course, sat in one of the 25. I didn't want to be different, not in the seventh grade! No one sat in those 10 chairs. When our teacher came in he told us that the only people allowed in those 10 chairs would be those students who earned "A" averages during the class. I thought, "Who cares?" Over the course of the next few weeks, a few students earned the "A" average required to sit in one of "those" chairs. My attitude remained unchanged.

It was about this time another teacher came in and inquired about the students in the 10 chairs. Our teacher started raving about these people and referring to them as "real brains." My attitude was starting to change. I wanted the teacher to talk about me like that! But I had to make an "A" average for that to happen. And so I did. What a motivator he was!

That is when I learned that we all have a sign on us that reads, "MAKE ME FEEL SPECIAL!" We all want to be praised and recognized for our efforts.

Take a tip from many of the top performers. When they are performing, they have the ability to make us feel like we are the only ones in the room.

That is the way we should make others feel when we are conversing with them. Too often you see conversations in which one person is always scanning the room to see who they are going to speak with next. Every person should get the "complete focus" treatment or it is a wasted conversation. Not paying attention creates a double loss. Not only did you probably learn nothing from the conversation, but you also conveyed in a non-verbal way what you thought of that other person.

Leaders know their success always comes down to how they treat others. True leaders help others to see themselves not just as they are currently, but also as what they can become.

Chapter 9

COMMUNICATION -- THE KEY TO DEVELOPING PERSONAL AND BUSINESS RELATIONSHIPS

Proper communication skills are critical to success in business, and to an even greater extent, life itself. At the heart of these skills lies the ability to verbalize your thoughts in a clear and concise manner. It is critical to understand that *how* you say something is just as important as *what* you say.

As an example, let's use the following statement: "I didn't say he wrecked his car." Each time you read this sentence, accent the word in italics and see how the same sentence changes meaning.

1.) *I* didn't say he wrecked his car.
This implies you didn't say it, but that everyone else is sure talking about it.

2.) I didn't *say* he wrecked his car.
Here you're conveying that while you didn't say it, you implied it and/or might have put in writing for others to read.

3.) I didn't say *he* wrecked his car.
No he didn't wreck it, but his wife turned it into a 3,000-pound paperweight.

4.) I didn't say he *wrecked* his car.
I wouldn't call it wrecked. It did flip over two or three times, but he drove it home.

5.) I didn't say he wrecked *his* car.
He wrecked his neighbor's car.

6.) I didn't say he wrecked his *car*.
His car is fine, but his boat is at the bottom of the ocean.

Clear communication is critical. If something is conveyed inaccurately, even if the correct words are used, it can be the beginning of a misunderstanding.

The following sample e-mail also demonstrates the ambiguous message that can be delivered if the communication is unclear:

Mike,

I know we are supposed to go out to dinner this evening, but I have other plans.

Karen

Hmm. How is Mike supposed to interpret this message? Maybe he is not confident is his relationship and interprets that Karen has plans with someone else. Does this mushroom in his mind to other negative thoughts? Is this the meaning of her message to him? Could it also mean that instead of going out as planned, she has an evening of passion in store for him?

Business is transacted around the world via e-mail at practically the speed of light. The opportunity for misunderstandings to occur becomes great. When you are communicating, especially through the written word, reread your letters and e-mails over a time or two to be sure the message you want to convey is the message your recipient will receive. Sorry, I don't know Mike or Karen, so I can't tell you how it turned out for them.

Another aspect of effective communication skills is being a good listener. We have to be good listeners to know how to properly respond and communicate with people.

If you need work in this area, here are a few ideas that can help you improve your listening skills:

1.) _Find at least one area of interest in what someone is saying._

Many times we may feel that after hearing a few

sentences, we're bored and think the person speaking couldn't possibly say anything we would find interesting. A good listener understands they can learn something from everyone.

2.) Listen for content, don't judge the package.

Don't immediately "size someone up" as a person who couldn't possibly say anything of interest. You probably don't like it when that is done to you, so give others a chance to share their thoughts.

For most of us, the best example of "sizing people up" as a criterion for listening would be going through a few introductions at a party. Do you remember the names of the people to whom you have been introduced? Do they remember yours? A friend of mine once said to me, "If people don't remember my name when we are introduced, I'm either mumbling or I'm boring. I make it a point to make an impression."

3.) Don't interrupt.

This one is so obvious I almost felt I shouldn't mention it. But so many people today have the very bad habit of interrupting others in mid-sentence, it became an important addition to the list.

4.) Resist distractions.

Listening properly means paying attention. It's not only rude to look around while someone else is speaking, it also makes it much more difficult to listen intently.

5.) Keep an open mind.

Ever hear the phrase, "He only hears what he wants to hear"? It's referring to a poor listener, someone who hears only selective comments. This happens for many reasons. Distractions or a lack of interest are two examples. It also occurs many times when someone "touches a nerve." As you read this you might be saying, "Wait a minute, when someone touches a nerve in me, it makes me really tune in!" Possibly, but only for the first moment. When a sensitive topic is discussed, most people begin thinking, "They can't say that!" This is usually when their listening stops and they begin thinking about how they are going to respond. I'm certainly not saying you have to agree with everyone, just keep an open mind and hear what he or she has to say.

6.) Work on your listening skills.

Listening is hard work. It takes focus. But

listening is how we learn. And the only way to improve our skills is to practice them with every conversation.

Power Principle
"When we are talking, we aren't learning."

Great communication skills also include many non-verbal areas, such as making proper eye contact. Making eye contact is important whether you are speaking with people individually, in small groups, or even in a large seminar venue. It shows people you are confident. Making eye contact when people are speaking to you conveys your interest in hearing what they have to say.

It may surprise you that other areas of non-verbal communication are punctuality and responsibility. These may seem unrelated to communication, however they communicate your image of yourself and what you think of other people.

Let's examine the most basic of communication skills, returning phone calls. In business, I believe you must make every effort to return all calls every day.

There are of course times when this is not

possible. For instance, when a message is left late in the day and you are out or tied-up in a meeting or conference. But there is no excuse for not returning that call the next business day. An option here would be to have your secretary or assistant return it, advising the other party of the reason for your delay. But at least make contact with the person who left the message. Most people will not mind a delay, as long as they know their message has been received and is being acknowledged.

When you don't return someone's call promptly, you are communicating his or her level of importance to you. After all, you probably return calls from your boss or upline manager pretty quickly. The same level of respect should be applied to every call you receive.

If you are late in returning someone's call, don't make excuses. Apologize and move on. To tell someone, "I have been very busy" is insulting. It is in essence saying, "Everything else in my life is more important than you." Hey, maybe that's true, but top-notch business people would never communicate that to others, either verbally or non-verbally. They always make others feel important.

If you promise to meet someone somewhere, be there and be on time! Here's an interesting little game you can play. Let's say you ask someone you know very well to meet you at a specific place one week from today at exactly 2 p.m. Now list everyone you know who, if asked, would be there *without* a reminder call from you during the week. Short list, huh? Do you think *you* would be on this list if one of your friends or associates were making it?

Being punctual and considerate of other's feelings is one of the most important ways to communicate your feelings to them.

Power Principle
"Great leaders are always great communicators!"

Great communicators don't burn their bridges. They know it's a small world and burning their bridges behind them is never a smart move. I can tell you from personal experience that every time I've found myself saying, "It's a small world," it's almost always followed by, "I'm glad I didn't burn that bridge."

That's because it always seems like the person you shun is the person who will inevitably be in a position to help you down the road.

Great communicators don't just ask better questions, they also care more about the answers they receive. They are always asking how they can help others and how they can improve as leaders, managers, and parents.

Great communication skills are the hallmark of most successful people. The key to receiving the respect of others is communicating your respect to them first.

Chapter 10

WHAT WILL YOU DO?

You should be applauded! You have taken the initiative to find this book and have nearly completed reading it. Now, what will you do?

The ideas contained in this book can help you make positive and powerful changes in your life. Will you take the initiative to make these changes?

If you're not motivated to change, nothing you read here will matter. I can share these strategies with you, but if you don't want to change, they will be virtually without meaning.

The reason for that is, I cannot motivate you. No one can. *You* have to want to be motivated. *You* have to want to win. This is something that can only come from inside you. No one else can do it but you!

If you want to improve the things *around* you, you must improve the things *within* you, first.

Let's face it, if achieving goals in life were easy, everyone would be doing just that. But the sad truth is, many people today don't even have goals. If you don't have goals of your own, you'll just end up helping others to achieve their goals while you go nowhere in life.

I have people tell me all the time, "I want to win, I want to succeed." But many are caught in what I call the Devil's Triangle. They get lost every night somewhere between the couch, the television and the refrigerator!

This is where many of the decisions that will shape your future are made. What will your response be to a great opportunity that comes knocking? Yes, make me rich, or leave me alone, I'm watching TV?

I believe that opportunity knocks all the time, but unless we are prepared and ready to receive these opportunities, they will just be wasted.

Remember, you can make excuses or progress, but not both. Some people will go through their entire lives doing nothing but making excuses.

It doesn't matter what business you are in, you will always run into people who have excuses why they can't follow through.

As an example, I've met many people who have told me they want to be wealthy. But quite a number of them would do it only if it didn't take too much work.

I truly believe that if I went to some of them with the key to Fort Knox in my hand and said, "The government said I could take all I want for the next 24 hours and I can bring a guest. Get a wheelbarrow and come with me!" I would probably hear the following. "Right now?" or "Do you know how much wheelbarrows cost?" or "Can you call me when you get the key again?"

I don't try to change people like that and neither should you. Just use the word I always use, "Next!" and then move on. Apply your energy to those who truly want to win.

Saying, "I want to win, I want to succeed," just isn't strong enough. Saying, "I *will* win, I *will* succeed!" is what it takes. You must have both strong desire and strong determination. Have the attitude that you will never quit. Never give up!

The difference between winning and losing is so small it's actually scary. Everyone wants to be successful and everyone wants to be special. A lot of people will do almost enough to win. But the odds are they are going to come up short. What will you do?

The winners in life do the extra things that non-winners won't. Winners write down their goals. They'll make a commitment to winning that knows no end, regardless of how long it takes.

Winners are not afraid to dream and try new things. They push themselves to new levels because they have causes to champion and are positive about their futures.

In short, a winner has an attitude, the attitude of a champion. And if *you* want that attitude, you can have it too.

Life is all about attitude. Our lives are going to turn out pretty much the way we envision them, so allow your positive attitude to dictate your destination. People who expect to fail usually do. People who expect to get sick every time someone comes in the office with a cold, usually do.

Have you ever had people tell you they were sick and tired of their jobs and the way their lives were turning out? Well, that's the beginning. When they get sick and tired of being sick and tired, when they get an attitude that they deserve better, that's when they will begin to win! Do you believe you deserve better? If not, you should.

Start expecting great things for yourself. Expect to be healthy. Expect success. Expect to win!

Most people don't pursue their dreams because they're afraid they might fail. Fear stops people from achieving what they want in life.

Power Principle
"Fear is the darkroom where negatives are developed."

Want to get rid of fear? Gain knowledge. With knowledge you have confidence, without it, you have fear.

While you are gaining this knowledge, get clear mental images of yourself achieving your dreams. Envision your life the way you want it to be. Then physically begin acting the part. I have heard this said a couple of ways: "Act the part and you become the part," or "Fake it 'til you make it."

Most people have attached such an ugly meaning to the word failure. But the truth is, failure is very important to success. Failure is never permanent, unless *you* decide it is! It's also true that if you have not failed at something recently, your life is probably too safe.

If that's the case, find new things to get excited about. Are you excited about your life every day? Are you one of those people who are anxious for Monday because you can't wait to see what the new week will bring into your life? If not, are you willing to make some changes that will help create that attitude? Do you want to change badly enough?

Try something new! You'll never fail if you make an *honest* attempt at success. Even if you try something and walk away with less than total success, you're stronger for doing so.

Find something to believe in. Find something to get excited about. Find a reason to be alive!

One of my favorite sayings is, "Yesterday is history, tomorrow is a mystery, and today is a gift from God, that's why we call it the present." Along with this "present," I believe God has given us another special gift. And it's our job to find out what that gift is and develop it to the best of our abilities.

Ask yourself, "What am I doing on this planet? What's *my* contribution to this life?" Life is all about choices. You either actively choose your own direction, or one is chosen for you through inaction.

Time is the most important commodity we have. And we spend it every day at a rate of 60 minutes per hour, 24 hours per day. We trade our time on this earth for what we believe is important. And it's not replaceable. So we had better be getting value all the time. We must make it count for something!

It's time to become a dreamer again. It's time to recognize and take advantage of the great opportunities you have been given.

This is where many adults can take a lesson from most children. Kids are dreamers by nature. But as many of us get older we lose that ability to dream. And the more we live lives without dreams, the closer we get to lives without meaning. Becoming a dreamer is the first step to increasing the possibility of success in your life. It is never too late to start dreaming. It's never too late to set goals and go after what you want.

If you think you are beaten, you are! If you think you can't win, you won't. If you think the odds are against you, they are! But if you want to win and be successful, you can. If you want to achieve your goals, you can! The bottom line is you can do it, but only if you want it badly enough.

Almost everyone wants to be on the "gravy train." You might even find that many on the train will reach out and help you to jump on. But at no point will people jump off the train to push you on board. Nor should they.

Well, it's decision time. It's time for you decide if you want to improve your life. The clock is ticking.

- Decide now to start dreaming again.
- Decide now to set goals and map out a strategy.
- Decide now to make an endless commitment to those dreams and goals.
- Decide now to push yourself to new levels.
- Decide now to be positive and excited about your life and the opportunities you have in front of you.

Make the most of this most precious of gifts, life! May all of your dreams come true.

Power Principle
"Get started now!"

Notes

Notes